TSW Publishing
P. O. Box 176
Centreville, Virginia 20122
www.scholarshipworkshop.com
TSW Publishing is a division of The Scholarship Workshop LLC

The Scholarship Monthly Planner was written to provide accurate advice to readers. However, please note that the author nor the publisher are engaged in the practice of providing legal, accounting, tax or other professional advice. If you need legal, accounting, tax or other advice, please consult a professional in the appropriate area. Neither the author, the publisher, nor any entity associated with *The Scholarship Monthly Planner* assume any liability for errors, omissions, or inaccuracies. Any action you take or do not take as a result of reading *The Scholarship Monthly Planner* is entirely your responsibility.

ISBN: 978-1-950653-52-2

Printed in the United States of America

This resource is available at special quantity discounts for bulk purchases for sales promotions, premiums, fundraising, and educational use. Special versions or excerpts can also be created to fit specific needs.

For more information, please contact info@scholarshipworkshop.com or call 703 579-4245. You can also write: TSW Publishing, P. O. Box 176, Centreville, Virginia 20122.

The Scholarship Monthly Planner
2025-2026

The Scholarship Monthly Planner

August 2025

SUN	MON	TUE	WED	THU	FRI	SAT
When visiting websites, you may need to use the search box on the site or through the home page to find the specific scholarship program listed.	Work on your scholarship résumé/extracurricular activity, honors, and awards list.	Look at all deadlines for upcoming scholarships you've already researched. Be sure they are included in your calendar.	*Check website for VFW Patriot's Pen Essay Contest rules — https://www.vfw.org/community/youth-and-education/youth-scholarships ———— Check website for application: Coca-Cola Scholars Foundation — https://www.coca-colascholarsfoundation.org/apply/	Ayn Rand "Atlas Shrugged" Essay Contest entry due AUGUST 1 — https://aynrand.org/students/essay-contests (open to 9th thru graduate school students) ———— Ayn Rand "Anthem" Essay Contest entry due AUGUST 1 — https://aynrand.org/students/essay-contests (open to 8th thru 12th grade students)	**1** Tylenol Future Care Scholarship Program application due — https://www.tylenol.com/tylenol-future-care-scholarship ———— Ayn Rand "Fountainhead" Essay Contest entry due — https://aynrand.org/students/essay-contests (open to 8th thru 12th grade students)	**2** Check website for Regeneron Science Talent Search process and rules — https://www.societyforscience.org/regeneron-sts/ ———— Check website for United States Senate Youth Program application process and regional deadlines — http://ussenateyouth.org
3 Check website for National YoungArts Foundation competition entry rules — www.youngarts.org ———— **Check website for Scholarship America Dream Award Application — https://learn-more.scholarsapply.org/dreamaward/	**4** Contact your local American Legion chapter for information on The American Legion National High School Oratorical Contest — www.legion.org	**5** *Check website for the ADHD College Success Scholarship Application — https://ncld.org/scholarships-awards	**6** Check website for entry rules: American Fire Sprinkler Association Second Chance Scholarship Contest — www.afsascholarship.org (FOR NONTRADITIONAL STUDENTS) Also see @afsascholarship or www.facebook.com/afsascholarship/	**7**	**8** Check website for Davidson Fellows Scholarship application process — http://www.davidsongifted.org/Fellows-Scholarship (OPEN TO ALL STUDENTS UNDER AGE 18)	**9** Check website for Gates Scholarship Application — https://www.thegatesscholarship.org/scholarship
10 Check website for QuestBridge National College Match application process — www.questbridge.org Also see www.facebook.com/questbridge	**11** +Check website for The Christophers Annual Video Contest — https://www.christophers.org/youth or https://www.christophers.org	**12** Check website for the Anne Ford Scholarship application — www.ncld.org	**13** ***Check website for Beinecke Scholarship nomination process — https://beineckescholarship.org	**14** **DO THIS NOW!** Review scholarship résumé/activity list for areas to improve such as community service, leadership, and overall involvement. A well-rounded student has a better chance of winning scholarships.	**15** Check website for entry kit: Toshiba NSTA ExploraVision Awards — www.exploravision.org (OPEN TO STUDENTS IN GRADES K—12)	**16** Check website for Soroptimist Live Your Dream Awards — https://www.soroptimist.org/our-work/live-your-dream-awards (OPEN TO WOMEN WHO ARE PRIMARY FINANICAL SUPPORT FOR THEIR HOUSEHOLD)
17 *Check website Don't Text and Drive Scholarship entry rules — www.digitalresponsibility.org/dont-text-and-drive-scholarship	**18** *+Check website for application: SMART Scholarship-for-Service Program — https://www.smartscholarship.org/smart	**19** Check with your student chapter advisor: DECA Scholarship Program — www.deca.org/scholarships	**20** Check website for Safe Driving Summer Scholarship — https://dosomething.org/action/100-for-100	**21** Check website for Gates Scholarship Application — https://www.thegatesscholarship.org/scholarship	**22** Check website for entry rules: American Fire Sprinkler Association High School Seniors Scholarship Contest — www.afsascholarship.org (FOR NONTRADITIONAL STUDENTS) Also see @afsascholarship or www.facebook.com/afsascholarship	**23** If you are a junior, start preparing for the PSAT which may be given by your high school in October. Your performance on this exam could qualify you for the National Merit Scholarship Competition.
24/31 Contact the National Society of the Daughters of the American Revolution (NSDAR) for information about their scholarship programs — www.dar.org or https://dar.academicworks.com	**25** Contact your local American Legion chapter for information on The American Legion National High School Oratorical Contest — www.legion.org	**26** Check website for Hispanic Heritage Youth Awards application — https://hispanicheritage.org/programs/leadership/youth-awards	**27** Check website for Chick-fil-A Community Scholarship — https://www.chick-fil-a.com/communityscholars	**28** Check website: Brave of Heart Scholarship Program application — https://learn-more.scholarsapply.org/braveofheart/	**29** Check website: Direct Textbook Essay Scholarship Opportunity — https://www.directtextbook.com/scholarship	**30** Safe Driving Summer Scholarship entry due — https://dosomething.org/action/100-for-100

The Scholarship Monthly Planner

Notes

_____
_____
_____
_____
_____
_____
_____
_____
_____
_____
_____
_____
_____
_____
_____
_____
_____
_____
_____
_____
_____
_____
_____
_____
_____
_____

DON'T FORGET!

- Final deadline dates have red text.
- Submit your application at least 7 days before the deadline.
- Always look at least 1 month ahead to get prepared for upcoming deadlines.
- Hate writing? Start on your essay at least 1 month prior to the deadline.
- Need recommendations? Ask at least 4 weeks prior to the deadline. Follow-up! Also, many programs request recommendations electronically. Please let someone know you've provided their e-mail address for a recommendation, so they will be prepared for the e-mail request.
- As you download applications, organize them. You should have one folder for each month. Place applications in the appropriate folder for each month. For example, all applications that are due in December should be in a folder marked December.
- Check previous months for application download dates or activities you need to complete. These activities are shown in black text. Although you may be behind with some activities, the deadline date for a scholarship or award may not have passed.
- Research and include local, regional, and state based scholarships in your calendar.
- Research and include scholarships based on your interests, personal characteristics, and situation in your calendar.
- Request nominations with a letter and your résumé.

The Scholarship Monthly Planner
September 2025

*Programs are open to current college students and high school seniors.

**Programs are open to current college students only.

***Programs are open to graduate and/or professional school students only.

+Program open to graduate and undergraduate students

Unless otherwise noted, all other programs are open to high school seniors.

SUN	MON	TUE	WED	THU	FRI	SAT
When visiting websites, you may need to use the search box on the site or scroll through the home page to find the specific scholarship program listed. *To get alerts of upcoming deadlines and new scholarship opportunities, like The Scholarship Workshop on Facebook or follow us @ScholarshipWork and @ScholarshipWorkshop on Instagram.* *You can also visit www.scholarshipworkshop.com/newsletter to join our mailing list for updates!*				Scan this QR code to visit our website for additional information and resources.	Check website for application: Elks Most Valuable Student Contest — https://www.elks.org/scholars/ or contact your local Elks lodge	Check website for application: Equitable Excellence Scholarship— https://equitable.com/foundation/equitable-excellence-scholarship
***Check website for GEM fellowship application— www.gemfellowship.org ——— Check website for rules: American Fire Sprinkler Association High School Senior Scholarship Contest — www.afsascholarship.org	1 American Fire Sprinkler Association Second Chance Scholarship Contest entry due — www.afsascholarship.org (FOR NONTRADITIONAL STUDENTS) Also see @afsascholarship or www.facebook.com/afsascholarship	2 Check website for application process and regional deadline: Junior Science and Humanities Symposium (JSHS) Program — www.jshs.org (OPEN TO GRADES 9 THRU 12)	3 **Check website for Scholarship America Dream Award Application — https://learn-more.scholarsapply.org/dreamaward/	4 Check website for Jack Kent Cooke College Scholarship Program application — www.jkcf.org	5 **Contact dean's office or department chair for nomination process: Coca-Cola Community College Academic Team Scholarship — www.ptk.org (See Scholarships)	6 Check website for application: Scholastic Art and Writing Awards — www.artandwriting.org (OPEN TO GRADES 7 THRU 12)
7 Contact your local American Legion chapter for information on The American Legion National High School Oratorical Contest — www.legion.org	8 Check website for The Christophers Annual Poster Contest — https://www.christophers.org/poster-contest or https://www.christophers.org (OPEN TO STUDENTS IN GRADES 9 THRU 12)	9 Check website for Ron Brown Scholarship application — www.ronbrown.org	10 Check website for Mu Alpha Theta Kalin Award nomination process — https://mualphatheta.org/kalin_award	11 Check website: Dr. Arnita Young Boswell Scholarship — www.nhbwinc.com or https://nhbwinc.org/scholarships	12 Direct Textbook Essay Scholarship Opportunity deadline — https://www.directtextbook.com/scholarship	13 Check website for C-Span's StudentCam competition — http://www.studentcam.org (OPEN TO STUDENTS IN GRADES 6 THRU 12)
14 Check website for application: Coca-Cola Scholars Foundation — www.coca-colascholarsfoundation.org	15 Gates Scholarship Application due — https://www.thegatesscholarship.org/scholarship	16 Check website for entry kit: Toshiba NSTA ExploraVision Awards — www.exploravision.org (OPEN TO STUDENTS IN GRADES K—12)	17 Check website for National Security Agency Stokes Educational Scholarship Program application — https://www.intelligencecareers.gov/NSA/students-and-internships	18 Check out College Board Opportunity Scholarships — https://bigfuture.collegeboard.org/pay-for-college/bigfuture-scholarships	19 Check website for Street Sweep Scholarship — https://dosomething.org/action/street-sweep	20 Check website for John F. Kennedy Profile in Courage Essay Contest rules — www.jfklibrary.org (OPEN TO GRADES 9 THRU 12
21 Check website for Unigo $10,000 Scholarship — https://www.unigo.com/scholarships/our-scholarships/unigo-10k-scholarship (OPEN TO STUDENTS AGE 14 AND UP)	22 *Check website for Create-A-Greeting-Card Scholarship Contest entry rules — www.gallerycollection.com/greetingcardscontests.htm (OPEN TO NONTRADITIONAL STUDENTS)	23 Consider applying early for the Equitable Excellence Scholarship (there may be an application limit)— https://equitable.com/foundation/equitable-excellence-scholarship	24 Check website for Regeneron Science Talent Search process and rules — https://student.societyforscience.org/regeneron-sts	25 QuestBridge National College Match application due soon — www.questbridge.org Also see www.facebook.com/questbridge	26 Check with your student chapter advisor: DECA Scholarship Program — www.deca.org/scholarships	27 Get a head start on college and scholarship essays with The Scholarship and College Essay Writing Boot Camp! See www.scholarshipworkshop.com or scan this QR Code.
28 *ADHD College Success Scholarship Application due — https://ncld.org/scholarships-awards	29 *Don't Text and Drive Scholarship deadline SEPTEMBER 30 — www.digitalresponsibility.org/dont-text-and-drive-scholarship/	30 Coca-Cola Scholarship application due — www.coca-colascholarsfoundation.org/	**ALERT!** Review scholarship résumé/activity list for areas to improve such as community service, leadership, and overall involvement. A well-rounded student has a better chance of winning scholarships.			

The Scholarship Monthly Planner

Notes

_____

_____

_____

_____

_____

_____

_____

_____

_____

_____

_____

_____

_____

_____

_____

_____

_____

_____

_____

_____

_____

_____

_____

_____

_____

_____

DON'T FORGET!

- Final deadline dates have red text.
- Submit your application at least 7 days before the deadline.
- Always look at least 1 month ahead to get prepared for upcoming deadlines.
- Hate writing? Start on your essay at least 1 month prior to the deadline.
- Need recommendations? Ask at least 4 weeks prior to the deadline. Follow-up! Also, many programs request recommendations electronically. Please let someone know you've provided their e-mail address for a recommendation, so they will be prepared for the e-mail request.
- As you download applications, organize them. You should have one folder for each month. Place applications in the appropriate folder for each month. For example, all applications that are due in December should be in a folder marked December.
- Check previous months for application download dates or activities you need to complete. These activities are shown in black text. Although you may be behind with some activities, the deadline date for a scholarship or award may not have passed.
- Research and include local, regional, and state based scholarships in your calendar.
- Research and include scholarships based on your interests, personal characteristics, and situation in your calendar.
- Request nominations with a letter and your résumé.

The Scholarship Monthly Planner
October 2025

*Programs are open to current college students and high school seniors.

**Programs are open to current college students only.

***Programs are open to graduate and/or professional school students only.

+Program open to graduate and undergraduate students

Unless otherwise noted, all other programs are open to high school seniors.

SUN	MON	TUE	WED	THU	FRI	SAT
	If you are a high school junior, get ready to take the PSAT this month. Scoring well among students in your state could qualify you for a National Merit scholarship.	Contact your local Optimist Club for information about the Optimist International Essay and Oratorical Contests — www.optimist.org or https://www.optimist.org/member/scholarships1.cfm (OPEN TO STUDENTS UNDER AGE 19)	**1** Check website for HRG Charitable Foundation Scholarship — https://scholarshipamerica.org/scholarship/hrg/	**2** Contact the National Society of the Daughters of the American Revolution (NSDAR) for information about their scholarship programs — www.dar.org or https://dar.academicworks.com	**3** ***Check website for GEM fellowship application— www.gemfellowship.org	**4** ***Contact your medical school's dean, student affairs or financial aid office to be considered for an AMA Foundation scholarship nomination — https://amafoundation.org/programs/scholarships
5 Check website: cg42 Foundation Scholarship — https://scholarshipamerica.org/scholarship/cg42foundation	**6** Check website: Stop Hunger Scholarship Program application and deadline — https://www.us.stop-hunger.org/grants/youth-scholarshipsor www.sodexofoundation.org (OPEN TO STUDENTS IN KINDERGARTEN THROUGH GRADUATE SCHOOL AGES 5 TO 25)	**7** National YoungArts Foundation competition entry due — www.youngarts.org	**8** If you're in NHS, confirm National Honor Society Scholarship Program verification process and deadline — www.nhs.us/scholarship	**9** Check website for Dell Scholarship Program application — www.dellscholars.org	**10** Get sponsor for — www.fra.org (see Events and Programs < Americanism Essay Contest) (OPEN TO GRADES 7 THRU 12) Deadline for sponsored entries December 1.	**11** Start working on your Free application for Federal Student Aid (FAFSA) — https://studentaid.gov/h/apply-for-aid/fafsa Also contact schools and states for their specific
12 Check out College Board Opportunity Scholarships — https://bigfuture.collegeboard.org/pay-for-college/bigfuture-scholarships	**13** Check website for application: Elks Most Valuable Student Contest — https://www.elks.org/scholars/ or contact your local Elks lodge	**14** **Check website for Jack Kent Cooke Undergraduate Transfer Scholarship application — www.jkcf.org	**15** Are you a female currently studying engineering, engineering technology and computer science ? If yes, visit this page for many opportunities through the Society of Women Engineers — https://swe.org/scholarships or www.swe.org (see Scholarships)	**16**	**17**	**18** Check website for application: Burger King Scholars Program — https://www.burgerkingfoundation.org/ or https://burger-king.scholarsapply.org
19 Check website for National Beta Club scholarship application — www.betaclub.org/scholarship	**20** *Check website for Essential Visionaries Scholarship Fund - https://scholarshipamerica.org/scholarship/essentialvisionaries	**21** **Check website for nomination process — All-USA Community College Academic Team — www.ptk.org (see Scholarships)	**22** Check website for FRA Foundation Scholarship applications —www.fra.org (see Events and Programs < Education Foundation Scholarships) (OPEN TO STUDENT FRA MEMBERS AFFILIATED WITH THE U.S. NAVY, MARINE CORPS OR COAST GUARD THEMSELVES OR THROUGH FAMILY MEMBER)	**23** Chick-fil-A Community Scholarship application due soon — https://www.chick-fil-a.com/communityscholars	**24** Marianne, $400,000 scholarship winner can take you step by step through the scholarship process in The Scholarship Boot Camp. Scan this QR code to learn more.	**25** Check website for rules: American Fire Sprinkler Association High School Seniors Scholarship Contest — www.afsascholarship.org
26	**27** Check website for entry rules: "Frame My Future" Scholarship Contest — www.framemyfuture.com or https://www.diplomaframe.com/contests/frame-my-future-scholarship.aspx	**28** Brave of Heart Scholarship Program application due — https://learn-more.scholarsapply.org/braveofheart/ or https://learn-more.scholarsapply.org/braveofheart/	**29** VFW Voice of Democracy Audio Essay Contest deadline—OCTOBER 31 — https://www.vfw.org/community/youth-and-education/youth-scholarships (OPEN TO GRADES 9 THRU 12)	**30** VFW Patriot's Pen Essay Contest entries due OCTOBER 31— https://www.vfw.org/community/youth-and-education/youth-scholarships (OPEN TO GRADES 6 THRU 8)	**31** National Security Agency Stokes Educational Scholarship Program application due — https://www.intelligencecareers.gov/NSA/students-and-internships STOKES MAY BE OFFERED BY OTHER GOVERNMENT AGENCIES.	

The Scholarship Monthly Planner

Notes

_____

_____

_____

_____

_____

_____

_____

_____

_____

_____

_____

_____

_____

_____

_____

_____

_____

_____

_____

_____

_____

_____

_____

_____

_____

_____

_____

DON'T FORGET!

- Final deadline dates have red text.
- Submit your application at least 7 days before the deadline.
- Always look at least 1 month ahead to get prepared for upcoming deadlines.
- Hate writing? Start on your essay at least 1 month prior to the deadline.
- Need recommendations? Ask at least 4 weeks prior to the deadline. Follow-up! Also, many programs request recommendations electronically. Please let someone know you've provided their e-mail address for a recommendation, so they will be prepared for the e-mail request.
- As you download applications, organize them. You should have one folder for each month. Place applications in the appropriate folder for each month. For example, all applications that are due in December should be in a folder marked December.
- Check previous months for application download dates or activities you need to complete. These activities are shown in black text. Although you may be behind with some activities, the deadline date for a scholarship or award may not have passed.
- Research and include local, regional, and state based scholarships in your calendar.
- Research and include scholarships based on your interests, personal characteristics, and situation in your calendar.
- Request nominations with a letter and your résumé.

The Scholarship Monthly Planner
November 2025

*Programs are open to current college students _and_ high school seniors.

**Programs are open to current college students only.

***Programs are open to graduate and/or professional school students only.

+Program open to graduate and undergraduate students

Unless otherwise noted, all other programs are open to high school seniors.

SUN	MON	TUE	WED	THU	FRI	SAT
+Check website for Alpha Kappa Alpha Educational Advancement Scholarship application — www.akaeaf.org	***Contact your medical school's dean, student affairs or financial aid office to be considered for an AMA Foundation Physicians of Tomorrow Scholarship nomination —https://amafoundation.org/programs/scholarships	Check website for application: Jackie Robinson Scholarship Program — www.jackierobinson.org	If you're in NHS, confirm National Honor Society Scholarship Program verification process and deadline — www.nhs.us/scholarship	*+Check website for William A. March Education Trust Scholarship — https://learn-more.scholarsapply.org/williammarchscholarship	Check website for Dell Scholarship Program application — www.dellscholars.org	**1** Check website for NHS Scholarship program application — www.nhs.us/scholarship
2 Hispanic Heritage Youth Awards application due — https://hispanicheritage.org/programs/leadership/youth-awards/	**3** **Check website for Wellroot Family Services Scholarship Program application — https://learn-more.scholarsapply.org/wellrootscholarship or https://scholarshipamerica.org/scholarship/wellrootscholarship	**4** Check website for Stockholm Junior Water Prize state competition entry forms — www.wef.org/SJWP/ (OPEN TO GRADES 9 THRU 12)	**5** +*Stop Hunger Scholarship Program deadline — www.sodexofoundation.org or https://www.us.stop-hunger.org/grants/youth-scholarships (OPEN TO STUDENTS IN KINDERGARTEN THROUGH GRADUATE SCHOOL AGES 5 TO 25)	**6** Regeneron Science Talent Search entry due — www.societyforscience.org/sts or https://student.societyforscience.org/regeneron-sts	**7** George S. & Stella M. Knight Essay Contest deadline soon — www.sar.org. Check with local chapters of Sons of the American Revolution for entry guidelines	**8** Check website for Ron Brown Scholarship application — www.ronbrown.org
9 Check website for application: DEWALT Trades Scholarship — https://learn-more.scholarsapply.org/dewalttrade (OPEN TO STUDENTS ATTENDING TWO-YEAR COLLEGE OR VOCATIONAL-TECHNICAL SCHOOLS)	**10** *Check website for Essential Visionaries Scholarship Fund - https://scholarshipamerica.org/scholarship/essentialvisionaries/	**11** Elks Most Valuable Student application due — https://www.elks.org/scholars/	**12** Jack Kent Cooke College Scholarship Program application due — https://www.jkcf.org/our-scholarships/college-scholarship-program/	**13** Check website for GE–Reagan Foundation Scholarship Program application — https://www.reaganfoundation.org/education/ge-reagan-foundation-scholarship Facebook page: https://www.facebook.com/GEReaganScholarships	**14** ***GEM fellowship application due — www.gemfellowship.org	**15** Soroptimist Live Your Dream Awards application due — https://www.soroptimist.org/our-work/live-your-dream-awards (OPEN TO WOMEN WHO ARE PRIMARY FINANCIAL SUPPORT FOR THEIR HOUSEHOLD)
16 *Check website for Create-A-Greeting-Card Scholarship Contest entry rules — www.gallerycollection.com/greetingcardscontests.htm (OPEN TO NONTRADITIONAL STUDENTS)	**17** *Check website for Taco Bell Live Mas Scholarship — https://www.tacobellfoundation.org/live-mas-scholarship (OPEN TO STUDENTS AGE 16 TO 26)	**18** Check website for SkyWater Foundation Scholarship application — https://learn-more.scholarsapply.org/skywater or https://scholarshipamerica.org/scholarship/skywater/	**19** Check website:: Amazon Future Engineer Scholarship application — https://scholarshipamerica.org/amazonfutureengineer/	**20** Check website for application: Jeanette Rankin Scholar Grant — www.rankinfoundation.org (OPEN TO WOMEN 35+)	**21** Check out College Board Opportunity Scholarships — https://opportunity.collegeboard.org/home	**22** Check website for American Water Scholarship — https://scholarshipamerica.org/scholarship/american-water/
23 +Check website for Progress of Ideas Scholarship application — https://learn-more.scholarsapply.org/schalkenbach or https://scholarshipamerica.org/scholarship/schalkenbach/	**24** **Check website for Ritchie-Jennings Memorial Scholarship application — www.acfe.com/scholarship.aspx	**25** Check website for TheDream.US National Scholarship Program application — https://www.thedream.us (FOR DREAMERS/DACA STUDENTS)	**26** If you haven't already, start working on your Free application for Federal Student Aid (FAFSA) — https://studentaid.gov/h/apply-for-aid/fafsa	**27** Check website: American Foreign Service Essay Contest entry rules — www.afsa.org/essaycontest	**28** Check website:: Women at Microsoft Scholarship — https://scholarshipamerica.org/scholarship/women-at-microsoft	**29** Check website for the Anne Ford Scholarship application — www.ncld.org —————— Check website for the Allegra Ford Thomas Scholarship application — www.ncld.org
30 Street Sweep Scholarship deadline — https://dosomething.org/action/street-sweep						

The Scholarship Monthly Planner

Notes

_____
_____
_____
_____
_____
_____
_____
_____
_____
_____
_____
_____
_____
_____
_____
_____
_____
_____
_____
_____
_____
_____
_____
_____

DON'T FORGET!

- Final deadline dates have red text.
- Submit your application at least 7 days before the deadline.
- Always look at least 1 month ahead to get prepared for upcoming deadlines.
- Hate writing? Start on your essay at least 1 month prior to the deadline.
- Need recommendations? Ask at least 4 weeks prior to the deadline. Follow-up! Also, many programs request recommendations electronically. Please let someone know you've provided their e-mail address for a recommendation, so they will be prepared for the e-mail request.
- As you download applications, organize them. You should have one folder for each month. Place applications in the appropriate folder for each month. For example, all applications that are due in December should be in a folder marked December.
- Check previous months for application download dates or activities you need to complete. These activities are shown in black text. Although you may be behind with some activities, the deadline date for a scholarship or award may not have passed.
- Research and include local, regional, and state based scholarships in your calendar.
- Research and include scholarships based on your interests, personal characteristics, and situation in your calendar.
- Request nominations with a letter and your résumé.

The Scholarship Monthly Planner
December 2025

*Programs are open to current college students and high school seniors.

**Programs are open to current college students only.

***Programs are open to graduate and/or professional school students only.

+Program open to graduate and undergraduate students

Unless otherwise noted, all other programs are open to high school seniors.

SUN	MON	TUE	WED	THU	FRI	SAT
				**Request application due date for Coca-Cola Community College Academic Team nomination team at your institution — www.ptk.org (see Scholarships)	+The Christophers Annual Video Contest entry due soon — https://www.christophers.org/video-contest-for-college-students or https://www.christophers.org/youth	Americanism Essay Contest entries due DECEMBER 1 — www.fra.org (see Events and Program < Americanism Essay Contest) (OPEN TO GRADES 7 THRU 12)
Dell Scholarship Program application due DECEMBER 1 — www.dellscholars.org	**1** Ron Brown Scholar application due — www.ronbrown.org	**2** Check website for The George S. & Stella M. Knight Essay Contest information and rules — www.sar.org (see Education) (OPEN TO GRADES 9 THRU 12)	**3** Burger King Scholars Program application due this month— https://www.burgerkingfoundation.org or https://burgerking.scholarsapply.org	**4** +Check website for American Association on Health & Disability Scholarship Program— https://www.aahd.us/initiatives/scholarship-program/ (OPEN TO STUDENTS WITH DISABILITIES)	**5** +SMART Scholarship Program application due — https://www.smartscholarship.org/smart	**6** Contact your local Executive Women International chapter for information on Adult Students in Scholastic Transition scholarship process — www.ewiconnect.com (OPEN TO ADULT STUDENTS)
7 *Check website for Dunkin' Baltimore/Metro DC Regional Scholarship — https://learn-more.scholarsapply.org/dunkinbaltimoredc or https://scholarshipamerica.org/scholarship/dunkinbaltimoredc	**8** **Scholarship America Dream Award Application due — https://learn-more.scholarsapply.org/dreamaward/	**9** Optimist International Essay and Oratorical Contests deadline in late December (contact local club for specific dates) — www.optimist.org (see Signature Programs) (OPEN TO STUDENTS UNDER AGE 19 AS OF 10/1/2025)	**10** Check website for The Joseph S. Rumbaugh Historical Oration Contest information and rules — www.sar.org (see Education) (OPEN TO GRADES 9 THRU 12)	**11** Check website for SkyWater Foundation Scholarship application — https://scholarshipamerica.org/scholarship/skywater/	**12** Check website for Mu Alpha Theta Scholarships — www.mualphatheta.org	**13** Contact your local Optimist Club for information about the Optimist International Essay and Oratorical Contests — www.optimist.org or https://www.optimist.org/member/scholarships1.cfm (OPEN TO STUDENTS UNDER AGE 19)
14 Equitable Excellence Scholarship application due soon (there may be an application limit so apply early)— https://equitable.com/foundation/equitable-excellence-scholarship	**15** Amazon Future Engineer Scholarship application due soon — https://scholarshipamerica.org/amazonfutureengineer/	**16** **Wellroot Family Services Scholarship Program application due — https://learn-more.scholarsapply.org/wellrootscholarship/	**17** Check website for DECA Scholarship Program application — www.deca.org/scholarships	**18** HRG Charitable Foundation Scholarship deadline — https://scholarshipamerica.org/scholarship/hrg/	**19** Use the Federal Student Aid Estimator to get an early estimate of your eligibility for federal student aid — https://studentaid.gov/aid-estimator/	**20** *Check website for application: Hispanic Scholarship Fund — www.hsf.net
21 Check website for Arthur M. & Berdena King Eagle Scout Contest rules — www.sar.org (see Education)	**22** Check website for Simon Youth Foundation Scholarship application — https://syf.org/scholarships/ Also see https://www.facebook.com/simonyouthfoundation	**23** Check out College Board Opportunity Scholarships — https://opportunity.collegeboard.org/home	**24** +Check website for application: Military Spouse Scholarships — https://www.militaryfamily.org/programs/spouses-scholarships (OPEN TO NONTRADITIONAL STUDENTS)	**25** Check out the Horatio Alger National Scholarship Application — www.horatioalger.org or https://scholars.horatioalger.org (OPEN TO HIGH SCHOOL JUNIORS)	**26** Check website for application: Scholarships for Military Children — www.militaryscholar.org or https://fisherhouse.org/programs/scholarship-programs	**27** Check website for rules: American Fire Sprinkler Association High School Senior Scholarship Contest — www.afsascholarship.org
28 Check website: cg42 Foundation Scholarship — https://scholarshipamerica.org/scholarship/cg42foundation	**29** Check website for entry rules: "Frame My Future" Scholarship Contest — www.framemyfuture.com or https://www.diplomaframe.com/contests/frame-my-future-scholarship.aspx	**30**	**31** Unigo $10,000 Scholarship entry due — https://www.unigo.com/scholarships/our-scholarships/unigo-10k-scholarship			

The Scholarship Monthly Planner

Notes

The Scholarship Monthly Planner
January 2026

*Programs are open to current college students and high school seniors.

**Programs are open to current college students only.

***Programs are open to graduate and/or professional school students only.

+Program open to graduate and undergraduate students

Unless otherwise noted, all other programs are open to high school seniors.

SUN	MON	TUE	WED	THU	FRI	SAT
			*Check website for Orphan Foundation of America Foster Care to Success scholarship application — https://www.fc2success.org/programs/scholarships-and-grants/	Check website for Mu Alpha Theta Scholarships — www.mualphatheta.org	Check website for Northwestern Mutual Childhood Cancer Survivor and Sibling Scholarship applications — https://learn-more.scholarsapply.org/nmsurvivors/	Contact the National Society of the Daughters of the American Revolution (NSDAR) for information about their scholarship programs — www.dar.org or https://dar.academicworks.com
National Beta Club scholarship application due soon — www.betaclub.org/scholarship	Check website for Cameron Impact Scholarship — https://www.bryancameroneducationfoundation.org This scholarship has an application limit. Apply early.	*Taco Bell Live Mas Scholarship submission due soon — https://www.tacobellfoundation.org/live-mas-scholarship/ (OPEN TO STUDENTS AGE 16 TO 26)	American Fire Sprinkler Association High School Senior Scholarship entry due JANUARY 1— www.afsascholarship.org Also see @afsascholarship and www.facebook.com/afsascholarship/	**1** GE–Reagan Foundation Scholarship Program application deadline soon— https://www.reaganfoundation.org/education/ge-reagan-foundation-scholarship or https://www.facebook.com/GEReaganScholarships	**2** **Check website for Wells Fargo Veterans scholarship program application — https://learn-more.scholarsapply.org/wellsfargoveterans or https://scholarshipamerica.org/scholarship/wellsfargoveterans/	**3** +Check website for Wireless History Foundation Scholarship application — https://scholarshipamerica.org/scholarship/whf/
4 *Check website for 100 Black Men Scholarship — www.100blackmen.org or https://100blackmen.org/program-activations/annual-scholarship-program or contact a local chapter	**5** Jackie Robinson scholarship application due — www.jackierobinson.org	**6** **Jack Kent Cooke Undergraduate Transfer Scholarship application due — www.jkcf.org	**7** Check website for application: Hispanic Scholarship Fund — www.hsf.net	**8** *+William A. March Education Trust Scholarship application due — https://learn-more.scholarsapply.org/williammarchscholarship	**9** DECA Scholarship Program application due — www.deca.org/scholarships	**10** Check website for application: Jeanette Rankin Scholar Grant — www.rankinfoundation.org (OPEN TO WOMEN 35+)
11 Contact your local Executive Women International chapter for information on EWISP scholarship process — www.ewiconnect.com	**12** If you haven't already, start working on your Free application for Federal Student Aid (FAFSA) — https://studentaid.gov Contact schools and states for their specific deadlines..	**13**	**14** Check website for Ruth Lilly and Dorothy Sargent Rosenberg Poetry Fellowships—https://www.poetryfoundation.org/awards/prizes-fellowship (OPEN TO NONTRADITIONAL STUDENTS)	**15** *Essential Visionaries Scholarship Fund application due JANUARY 16 - https://scholarshipamerica.org/scholarship/essentialvisionaries/	**16** John F. Kennedy Profile in Courage Essay Contest entry due — www.jfklibrary.org/ (OPEN TO GRADES 9 THRU 12)	**17**
18 Check website for Doodle 4 Google entry rules and deadline— www.google.com/doodle4google (OPEN TO STUDENTS IN KINDERGARTEN THRU 12)	**19** *Check website for Steiner Family Scholarship — https://learn-more.scholarsapply.org/steinerfamilyscholarship (OPEN TO STUDENTS IN US AND CANADA)	**20** C-Span's StudentCam competition deadline — http://www.studentcam.org (OPEN TO STUDENTS IN GRADES 6 THRU 12)	**21** Check website: Dr. Arnita Young Boswell Scholarship — www.nhbwinc.com or https://nhbwinc.org/scholarships	**22**	**23** *+Check website for Dr. Angela E. Grant Memorial Scholarship deadline—http://drangelagrantscholarship.org (OPEN TO CANCER SURVIVORS OR THOSE WITH IMMEDIATE FAMILY MEMBERS DIAGNOSED WITH CANCER)	**24** Check out College Board Opportunity Scholarships — https://opportunity.collegeboard.org/home
25 Check website for Gloria Barron Prize for Young Heroes application — https://barronprize.org/apply (OPEN TO STUDENTS AGE 8 TO 18)	**26**	**27** Toshiba NSTA ExploraVision Awards application due soon — www.exploravision.org (OPEN TO STUDENTS IN GRADES K—12)	**28**	**29** National Society of the Daughters of the American Revolution (NSDAR) scholarship application due JANUARY 31 — www.dar.org or https://dar.academicworks.com	**30** +Progress of Ideas Scholarship application due — https://scholarshipamerica.org/scholarship/schalkenbach/	**31**

The Scholarship Monthly Planner

Notes

_____

_____

_____

_____

_____

_____

_____

_____

_____

_____

_____

_____

_____

_____

_____

_____

_____

_____

_____

_____

_____

_____

_____

_____

_____

DON'T FORGET!

- Final deadline dates have red text.
- Submit your application at least 7 days before the deadline.
- Always look at least 1 month ahead to get prepared for upcoming deadlines.
- Hate writing? Start on your essay at least 1 month prior to the deadline.
- Need recommendations? Ask at least 4 weeks prior to the deadline. Follow-up! Also, many programs request recommendations electronically. Please let someone know you've provided their e-mail address for a recommendation, so they will be prepared for the e-mail request.
- As you download applications, organize them. You should have one folder for each month. Place applications in the appropriate folder for each month. For example, all applications that are due in December should be in a folder marked December.
- Check previous months for application download dates or activities you need to complete. These activities are shown in black text. Although you may be behind with some activities, the deadline date for a scholarship or award may not have passed.
- Research and include local, regional, and state based scholarships in your calendar.
- Research and include scholarships based on your interests, personal characteristics, and situation in your calendar.
- Request nominations with a letter and your résumé.

The Scholarship Monthly Planner
February 2026

*Programs are open to current college students and high school seniors.

**Programs are open to current college students only.

***Programs are open to graduate and/or professional school students only.

+Program open to graduate and undergraduate students

Unless otherwise noted, all other programs are open to high school seniors.

SUN	MON	TUE	WED	THU	FRI	SAT
						The Christophers Annual Poster Contest deadline this month — https://www.christophers.org/poster-contest or https://www.christophers.org/youth
1 *Mu Alpha Theta Scholarship application due FEBRUARY 2 — www.mualphatheta.org	**2** **Ritchie-Jennings Memorial Scholarship application due — www.acfe.com/scholarship.aspx	**3** Entry due soon for Davidson Fellows Scholarship application process — http://www.davidsongifted.org/Fellows-Scholarship (OPEN TO ALL STUDENTS UNDER AGE 18)	**4**	**5** American Foreign Service Essay Contest entry due soon — www.afsa.org/essaycontest/	**6** Check website for Cameron Impact Scholarship — https://www.bryancameronducationfoundation.org This scholarship has an application limit. Apply early.	**7** +Check website for International Bridge, Tunnel and Turnpike Association Scholarship Program application — https://www.ibtta.org/ibtta-foundation-scholarship-program or https://scholarshipamerica.org/scholarship/ibtta/
8	**9** Check website for Jack Kent Cooke Young Scholars Program application — https://www.jkcf.org/our-scholarships/young-scholars-program/ (OPEN TO 7TH GRADE STUDENTS ONLY)	**10** Simon Youth Foundation Scholarship application due soon — https://syf.org/scholarships/ Also see https://www.facebook.com/simonyouthfoundation	**11** Scholarships for Military Children application due soon — https://militaryscholar.org or https://fisherhouse.org/programs/scholarship-programs	**12**	**13** Jeanette Rankin Women's Scholarship Fund application due www.rankinfoundation.org (OPEN TO WOMEN 35 AND UP)	**14** *+Hispanic Scholarship Fund application due — www.hsf.net
15 Check website for Jack Kent Cooke Young Scholars Program application — https://www.jkcf.org/our-scholarships/young-scholars-program/ (OPEN TO 7TH GRADE STUDENTS ONLY)	**16** *Check website for Central Intelligence Agency (CIA) **Undergraduate** Scholarship Program application — https://www.cia.gov/careers/student-programs/	**17** ***Check website for Central Intelligence Agency (CIA) **Graduate Studies** Scholarship Program application — https://www.cia.gov/careers/student-programs/	**18** **Check website—National Association for Campus Activities for scholarship opportunities — https://www.naca.org/FOUNDATION/Pages/Scholarships.aspx	**19** **Check website for The Voyager Scholarship, The Obama-Chesky Scholarship for Public Service application — https://www.obama.org/voyager-scholarship/	**20** Check website for Super Power Scholarship — https://www.unigo.com/scholarships/our-scholarships/superpower-scholarship (OPEN TO STUDENTS AGE 14 AND UP)	**21** Check website for Horatio Alger Career & Technical Scholarship Program Application — www.horatioalger.org or https://scholars.horatioalger.org (MUST BE HIGH SCHOOL GRADUATE ENROLLED IN AN ASSOCIATE'S DEGREE, CERTIFICATE, OR DIPLOMA PROGRAM)
22 Submission deadline soon for Ruth Lilly and Dorothy Sargent Rosenberg Poetry Fellowships —https://www.poetryfoundation.org/awards/prizes-fellowship (OPEN TO NONTRADITIONAL STUDENTS)	**23** TheDream.US National Scholarship Program application due soon—https://www.thedream.us (FOR DREAMERS/DACA STUDENTS)	**24** cg42 Foundation Scholarship deadline— https://scholarshipamerica.org/scholarship/cg42foundation	**25** American Foreign Service Essay Contest entry due soon — www.afsa.org/essaycontest	**26** Check website for Doodle 4 Google entry rules —www.google.com/doodle4google (OPEN TO STUDENTS IN KINDERGARTEN THRU 12)	**27** *Check website for Dunkin' Baltimore/Metro DC Regional Scholarship — https://learnmore.scholarsapply.org/dunkinbaltimoredc or https://scholarshipamerica.org/scholarship/dunkinbaltimoredc	**28**

The Scholarship Monthly Planner

Notes

_____
_____
_____
_____
_____
_____
_____
_____
_____
_____
_____
_____
_____
_____
_____
_____
_____
_____
_____
_____
_____
_____
_____
_____
_____
_____
_____
_____

DON'T FORGET!

- Final deadline dates have red text.
- Submit your application at least 7 days before the deadline.
- Always look at least 1 month ahead to get prepared for upcoming deadlines.
- Hate writing? Start on your essay at least 1 month prior to the deadline.
- Need recommendations? Ask at least 4 weeks prior to the deadline. Follow-up! Also, many programs request recommendations electronically. Please let someone know you've provided their e-mail address for a recommendation, so they will be prepared for the e-mail request.
- As you download applications, organize them. You should have one folder for each month. Place applications in the appropriate folder for each month. For example, all applications that are due in December should be in a folder marked December.
- Check previous months for application download dates or activities you need to complete. These activities are shown in black text. Although you may be behind with some activities, the deadline date for a scholarship or award may not have passed.
- Research and include local, regional, and state based scholarships in your calendar.
- Research and include scholarships based on your interests, personal characteristics, and situation in your calendar.
- Request nominations with a letter and your résumé.

The Scholarship Monthly Planner
March 2026

*Programs are open to current college students and high school seniors.

**Programs are open to current college students only.

***Programs are open to graduate and/or professional school students only.

+Program open to graduate and undergraduate students

Unless otherwise noted, all other programs are open to high school seniors.

SUN	MON	TUE	WED	THU	FRI	SAT
				Begin looking for local scholarship and award opportunities. Many may have deadlines in this month or later. To learn more about finding local opportunities, see the chapter, "The Local Scholarship Search: Finding Scholarships in Your Backyard" in *Winning Scholarships for College*, 5th or later edition.	Check for various Ayn Rand Essay Contest deadlines — www.aynrand.org or www.aynrand.org/students/essay-contests (OPEN TO STUDENTS AGE 13+ INCLUDING COLLEGE STUDENTS, AND GRADUATE STUDENTS)	Leading the Future II Scholarship application due — www.scholarshipworkshop.com
1 Horatio Alger National Scholarship Application due — www.horatioalger.org or https://scholars.horatioalger.org (OPEN TO HIGH SCHOOL JUNIORS)	2 Doodle 4 Google entry due soon — www.google.com/doodle4google (OPEN TO STUDENTS IN KINDERGARTEN THRU 12)	3 DEWALT Trades Scholarship deadline — https://learnmore.scholarsapply.org/dewalttrade/ (OPEN TO STUDENTS ATTENDING TWO-YEAR COLLEGE OR VOCATIONAL-TECHNICAL SCHOOLS)	4 Steiner Family Scholarship application due — https://scholarshipamerica.org/scholarship/steinerfamilyscholarship/ (OPEN TO STUDENTS IN US AND CANADA)	5 Check website for Wells Fargo Stacey Milbern Scholarship Program for People with Disabilities application — https://learnmore.scholarsapply.org/pwdscholarship	6 American Association on Health & Disability Scholarship Program application due—https://www.aahd.us/initiatives/scholarship-program/ (OPEN TO STUDENTS WITH DISABILITIES)	7 Check website for Military Commanders' Scholarship application — https://learnmore.scholarsapply.org/militarycommanders or www.militarycommandersscholarship.org
8 "Frame My Future" Scholarship Contest deadline soon — www.framemyfuture.com or https://www.diplomaframe.com/contests/frame-my-future-scholarship.aspx	9 *Create-A-Greeting-Card Scholarship Contest entry due — www.gallerycollection.com/greetingcardscontests.htm (OPEN TO NONTRADITIONAL and INTERNA-	10 **Complete Wells Fargo Veterans Scholarship application — https://learnmore.scholarsapply.org/wellsfargoveterans/ (APPLY EARLY. FUNDS CAN RUN OUT)	11	12	13	14
15 *Check website for Shawn Carter Scholarship — www.shawncartersf.com	16 Women at Microsoft Scholarship deadline — https://scholarshipamerica.org/scholarship/women-at-microsoft	17	18 American Water Inclusion and Diversity Scholarship application due soon — https://scholarshipamerica.org/scholarship/american-water/	19 The Voyager Scholarship, The Obama-Chesky Scholarship for Public Service application due soon — https://www.obama.org/programs/voyager-scholarship/	20 Start working on your outfit for the Stuck at Prom Contest — www.stuckatprom.com	21
22	23	24 Anne Ford Scholarship application due soon — www.ncld.org (OPEN TO STUDENTS WITH LEARNING DISABILITIES) ———— Allegra Ford Thomas Scholarship application due soon— www.ncld.org (OPEN TO STUDENTS WITH LEARNING DISABILITIES)	25	26 SkyWater Foundation Scholarship application due soon — https://scholarshipamerica.org/scholarship/skywater/	27 ***Deadline for Beinecke Scholarship nomination — http://fdnweb.org/beinecke/	28
29	30	31 Super Power Scholarship deadline — https://www.unigo.com/scholarships/our-scholarships/superpower-scholarship (OPEN TO STUDENTS AGE 14 AND UP)				

The Scholarship Monthly Planner

Notes

The Scholarship Monthly Planner
April 2026

*Programs are open to current college students and high school seniors.

**Programs are open to current college students only.

***Programs are open to graduate and/or professional school students only.

+Program open to graduate and undergraduate students

Unless otherwise noted, all other programs are open to high school seniors.

SUN	MON	TUE	WED	THU	FRI	SAT
					National scholarship and award deadlines will decline significantly after this month. If you haven't already, begin intensive research for community and state based scholarships and awards. Consider reading *Last Minute College Financing Guide*.	Use this QR code to learn more about *Last Minute College Financing Guide*.
			1 *Check website for Pega Scholars Program application — https://learn-more.scholarsapply.org/pegascholars/ (APPLICATION LIMIT OF 150. APPLY EARLY. ALSO AVAILABLE TO INTERNATIONAL STUDENTS FROM CERTAIN COUNTRIES)	**2** Check website for Horatio Alger Career & Technical Scholarship Program Application — www.horatioalger.org or https://scholars.horatioalger.org	**3** *Check website for Shawn Carter Scholarship — www.shawncartersf.com	**4** .*Check website for Central Intelligence Agency (CIA) **Undergraduate** Scholarship Program application — https://www.cia.gov/careers/student-programs/
5 ***Check website for Central Intelligence Agency (CIA) **Graduate** Scholarship Program application — https://www.cia.gov/careers/jobs/graduate-scholarship-program/	**6** Check website for Do-Over Scholarship — https://www.unigo.com/scholarships/our-scholarships/do-over-scholarship (OPEN TO STUDENTS AGE 13 AND UP)	**7** Jack Kent Cooke Young Scholars Program application due soon — www.jkcf.org/scholarships (OPEN TO 7TH GRADE STUDENTS ONLY)	**8**	**9** Check website for Cameron Impact Scholarship early deadline — https://www.bryancameroneducationfoundation.org This scholarship has an application limit so apply early!	**10**	**11**
12	**13** FRA Foundation Scholarship applications due APRIL 15 — www.fra.org (see Events and Programs < Education Foundation Scholarships) (OPEN TO STUDENT FRA MEMBERS AFFILIATED WITH THE U.S. NAVY, MARINE CORPS OR COAST GUARD THEMSELVES OR THROUGH FAMILY MEMBER)	**14** +Alpha Kappa Alpha Educational Advancement Scholarship applications due APRIL 15 — www.akaeaf.org ——— +Wireless History Foundation Scholarship application due — https://scholarshipamerica.org/scholarship/whf/	**15** *Dunkin' Baltimore/Metro DC Regional Scholarship application due — https://scholarshipamerica.org/scholarship/dunkinbaltimoredc Gloria Barron Prize for Young Heroes application due APRIL 15— https://barronprize.org/apply (OPEN TO STUDENTS AGE 8 TO 18)	**16**	**17** Wells Fargo Stacey Milbern Scholarship Program for People with Disabilities application due soon — https://learn-more.scholarsapply.org/pwdscholarship/	**18**
19	**20** +International Bridge, Tunnel and Turnpike Association Scholarship Program application due — https://www.ibtta.org/ibtta-foundation-scholarship-program	**21**	**22**	**23**	**24** Start working on your outfit for the Stuck at Prom Contest — www.stuckatprom.com	**25**
26	**27**	**28**	**29** *Shawn Carter Scholarship application due APRIL 30 — www.shawncartersf.com Also see www.facebook.com/SCScholarship and	**30** *** Ragins/Braswell National Scholarship application due — www.scholarshipworkshop.com		

The Scholarship Monthly Planner

Notes

_____
_____
_____
_____
_____
_____
_____
_____
_____
_____
_____
_____
_____
_____
_____
_____
_____
_____
_____
_____
_____
_____
_____

DON'T FORGET!

- Final deadline dates have red text.
- Submit your application at least 7 days before the deadline.
- Always look at least 1 month ahead to get prepared for upcoming deadlines.
- Hate writing? Start on your essay at least 1 month prior to the deadline.
- Need recommendations? Ask at least 4 weeks prior to the deadline. Follow-up! Also, many programs request recommendations electronically. Please let someone know you've provided their e-mail address for a recommendation, so they will be prepared for the e-mail request.
- As you download applications, organize them. You should have one folder for each month. Place applications in the appropriate folder for each month. For example, all applications that are due in December should be in a folder marked December.
- Check previous months for application download dates or activities you need to complete. These activities are shown in black text. Although you may be behind with some activities, the deadline date for a scholarship or award may not have passed.
- Research and include local, regional, and state based scholarships in your calendar.
- Research and include scholarships based on your interests, personal characteristics, and situation in your calendar.
- Request nominations with a letter and your résumé.

The Scholarship Monthly Planner
May 2026

*Programs are open to current college students and high school seniors.

**Programs are open to current college students only.

***Programs are open to graduate and/or professional school students only.

+Program open to graduate and undergraduate students

Unless otherwise noted, all other programs are open to high school seniors.

SUN	MON	TUE	WED	THU	FRI	SAT
			National scholarship and award deadlines usually decline in the late spring and summer. If you haven't already, begin intensive research for community and state based scholarships and awards. Consider reading *Last Minute College Financing Guide*.	Use this QR code to learn more about *Last Minute College Financing Guide*.	**1** *+Dr. Angela E. Grant Memorial Scholarship deadline — http:// drangelagrantscholarship.org (OPEN TO CANCER SURVIVORS OR THOSE WITH IMMEDIATE FAMILY MEMBERS DIAGNOSED WITH CANCER)	**2** **Check website for application: Tylenol Future Care Scholarship Program — https:// www.tylenol.com/ tylenol-future-care-scholarship
3	**4** Check for local scholarship deadlines. One student who worked with Marianne Ragins applied for a $1000 local scholarship with a deadline on May 15 and won it within 2 weeks. To learn more about finding local scholarship opportunities, see the chapter, "The Local Scholarship Search: Finding Scholarships in Your Backyard" in *Winning Scholarships for College*, 5th or later edition.	**5**	**6**	**7**	**8**	**9**
10	**11**	**12**	**13**	**14**	**15**	**16** *+Check website for DoSomething.org Easy Scholarships — https:// dosomething.org/pays -to-do-good or www.dosomething.org *(see Pays to Do Good)* This site has various scholarships with deadlines usually at the beginning or end of the month.
17	**18**	**19** Horatio Alger Career & Technical Scholarship Program Application due soon — https:// scholars.horatioalger.org/ about-our-scholarship-programs/technical	**20**	**21**	**22** +Complete Military Spouse Scholarship application (awards made quarterly)— www.militaryfamily.org or https:// www.militaryfamily.org/programs/ spouses-scholarships/ (OPEN TO NONTRADITIONAL STUDENTS)	**23**
24	**25**	**26**	**27**	**28**	**29**	**30**
31						

The Scholarship Monthly Planner

Notes

_____
_____
_____
_____
_____
_____
_____
_____
_____
_____
_____
_____
_____
_____
_____
_____
_____
_____
_____
_____
_____
_____
_____
_____
_____
_____

DON'T FORGET!

- Final deadline dates have red text.
- Submit your application at least 7 days before the deadline.
- Always look at least 1 month ahead to get prepared for upcoming deadlines.
- Hate writing? Start on your essay at least 1 month prior to the deadline.
- Need recommendations? Ask at least 4 weeks prior to the deadline. Follow-up! Also, many programs request recommendations electronically. Please let someone know you've provided their e-mail address for a recommendation, so they will be prepared for the e-mail request.
- As you download applications, organize them. You should have one folder for each month. Place applications in the appropriate folder for each month. For example, all applications that are due in December should be in a folder marked December.
- Check previous months for application download dates or activities you need to complete. These activities are shown in black text. Although you may be behind with some activities, the deadline date for a scholarship or award may not have passed.
- Research and include local, regional, and state based scholarships in your calendar.
- Research and include scholarships based on your interests, personal characteristics, and situation in your calendar.
- Request nominations with a letter and your résumé.

The Scholarship Monthly Planner
June 2026

*Programs are open to current college students and high school seniors.

**Programs are open to current college students only.

***Programs are open to graduate and/or professional school students only.

+Program open to graduate and undergraduate students

Unless otherwise noted, all other programs are open to high school seniors.

SUN	MON	TUE	WED	THU	FRI	SAT
	National scholarship and award deadlines usually decline in the late spring and summer. If you haven't already, begin intensive research for community and state based scholarships and awards. Consider reading *Last Minute College Financing Guide*.		IF YOU JUST STARTED USING THIS EDITION OF *THE SCHOLARSHIP MONTHLY PLANNER*, WE HAVE A PREPUBLICATION DISCOUNT ON *THE SCHOLARSHIP MONTHLY PLANNER* FOR THE **2026-2027 ACADEMIC YEAR DUE IN AUGUST 2026**, PLEASE CONTACT THE SCHOLARSHIP WORKSHOP AT info@scholarshipworkshop.com for more details.			
Stuck at Prom Contest entries due this month — www.stuckatprom.com Check website for official rules.	1	2	3 **Check website— National Association for Campus Activities for scholarship opportunities— https://www.naca.org/ FOUNDATION/Pages/ Scholarships.aspx	4	5 **Check website for application: Tylenol Future Care Scholarship Program — https:// www.tylenol.com/ tylenol-future-care-scholarship	6
7	8	9	10	11	12 ***Central Intelligence Agency (CIA) Graduate Studies Scholarship Program application due soon — https://www.cia.gov/ careers/student-programs/	13 *Central Intelligence Agency (CIA) Undergraduate Scholarship Program application due soon — https://www.cia.gov/ careers/student-programs/
14	15	16 Begin working on Ayn Rand Essay Contest entries — https://aynrand.org/ students/essay-contests	17	18	19 *+Check website for DoSomething.org Easy Scholarships — https:// dosomething.org/pays-to-do-good or www.dosomething.org *(see Pays to Do Good)* This site has various scholarships with deadlines usually at the beginning or end of the month.	20
21	22	23	24	25	26	27
28	29	30				

The Scholarship Monthly Planner

Notes

_____
_____
_____
_____
_____
_____
_____
_____
_____
_____
_____
_____
_____
_____
_____
_____
_____
_____
_____
_____
_____
_____
_____
_____
_____
_____
_____
_____
_____
_____

DON'T FORGET!

- Final deadline dates have red text.
- Submit your application at least 7 days before the deadline.
- Always look at least 1 month ahead to get prepared for upcoming deadlines.
- Hate writing? Start on your essay at least 1 month prior to the deadline.
- Need recommendations? Ask at least 4 weeks prior to the deadline. Follow-up! Also, many programs request recommendations electronically. Please let someone know you've provided their e-mail address for a recommendation, so they will be prepared for the e-mail request.
- As you download applications, organize them. You should have one folder for each month. Place applications in the appropriate folder for each month. For example, all applications that are due in December should be in a folder marked December.
- Check previous months for application download dates or activities you need to complete. These activities are shown in black text. Although you may be behind with some activities, the deadline date for a scholarship or award may not have passed.
- Research and include local, regional, and state based scholarships in your calendar.
- Research and include scholarships based on your interests, personal characteristics, and situation in your calendar.
- Request nominations with a letter and your résumé.

The Scholarship Monthly Planner

July 2026

SUN	MON	TUE	WED	THU	FRI	SAT
National scholarship and award deadlines usually decline in the late spring and summer. If you haven't already, begin intensive research for community and state based scholarships and awards. Consider reading the *Last Minute College Financing Guide*.	Use this QR code to learn more about *Last Minute College Financing Guide*.		IF YOU JUST STARTED USING THIS EDITION OF *THE SCHOLARSHIP MONTHLY PLANNER,* WE HAVE A PREPUBLICATION DISCOUNT ON *THE SCHOLARSHIP MONTHLY PLANNER* FOR THE 2026-2027 ACADEMIC YEAR DUE IN AUGUST 2027, PLEASE CONTACT THE SCHOLARSHIP WORKSHOP AT info@scholarshipworkshop.com for more details.	If you will be a college freshman in the upcoming academic year, get ready now for upcoming August deadlines and activities.	Check out *Scholarships for College Students* on Amazon. This book is helpful for rising college freshmen and current college students..	Current college students should research associations and organizations related to their major or minor for scholarship and award opportunities.
			1	**2**	**3**	**4**
5	**6** Begin working on Ayn Rand Essay Contest entries — https://aynrand.org/students/essay-contests	**7**	**8** Graduate and professional school students should research government agencies and research oriented companies in need of individuals from their study area.	**9**	**10** * Pega Scholars Program application due soon — https://learn-more.scholarsapply.org/pegascholars/ (APPLICATION LIMIT OF 150. APPLY EARLY. ALSO AVAILABLE TO INTERNATIONAL STUDENTS FROM CERTAIN COUNTRIES)	**11**
12	**13**	**14**	**15**	**16**	**17**	**18**
19	**20**	**21** *+Check website for DoSomething.org Easy Scholarships — https://dosomething.org/pays-to-do-good or www.dosomething.org *(see Pays to Do Good)* This site has various scholarships with deadlines usually at the beginning or end of the month.	**22**	**23** Review *Scholarships for College Students* — a guide to help current college students find and win scholarship money.. See www.scholarshipworkshop.com/bookstore	**24**	**25**
26	**27**	**28**	**29**	**30**	**31**	

*Programs are open to current college students and high school seniors.

**Programs are open to current college students only.

***Programs are open to graduate and/or professional school students only.

+Program open to graduate and undergraduate students

Unless otherwise noted, all other programs are open to high school seniors.

The Scholarship Monthly Planner

Notes

_____
_____
_____
_____
_____
_____
_____
_____
_____
_____
_____
_____
_____
_____
_____
_____
_____
_____
_____
_____
_____
_____
_____
_____
_____

DON'T FORGET!

- Final deadline dates have red text.
- Submit your application at least 7 days before the deadline.
- Always look at least 1 month ahead to get prepared for upcoming deadlines.
- Hate writing? Start on your essay at least 1 month prior to the deadline.
- Need recommendations? Ask at least 4 weeks prior to the deadline. Follow-up! Also, many programs request recommendations electronically. Please let someone know you've provided their e-mail address for a recommendation, so they will be prepared for the e-mail request.
- As you download applications, organize them. You should have one folder for each month. Place applications in the appropriate folder for each month. For example, all applications that are due in December should be in a folder marked December.
- Check previous months for application download dates or activities you need to complete. These activities are shown in black text. Although you may be behind with some activities, the deadline date for a scholarship or award may not have passed.
- Research and include local, regional, and state based scholarships in your calendar.
- Research and include scholarships based on your interests, personal characteristics, and situation in your calendar.
- Request nominations with a letter and your résumé.

The Scholarship Monthly Planner

Important Notes & Reminders

- The scholarship programs and awards shown in *The Scholarship Monthly Planner* may not represent all scholarships available to you. Those listed are generally available to a majority of students. Please conduct additional research to find scholarships in your community and state as well as those that apply to your situation and specific interests. To learn how to find additional scholarships, read *Winning Scholarships for College* or attend a workshop or online class conducted by Marianne Ragins. You can also visit www.scholarshipworkshop.com and refer to the scholarship search or scholarship help section as well as the books and resources section for more information about online searches.

- Deadline dates may have changed prior to or after the publication of *The Scholarship Monthly Planner*. Please use the information provided to check the most current deadline date. In some cases, the prior year's date may be included to give an approximate timeframe for the current year's deadline.

- Scholarship and award programs may be discontinued at any time.

- Some programs and awards included in the planner require nominations before you can submit an application. Use the contact information to find out to how to be nominated for a scholarship or award. For more information on requesting nominations, read *Winning Scholarships for College,* which includes a nomination request letter and other information.

- Some dates in the planner list more than one scholarship or award program.

- All text in red indicates a scholarship or award deadline. Space does not allow indication of whether this is a postmark or receipt date. To ensure your application or entry is received within the appropriate timeframe, please visit the website shown for more information and submit your application at least 7 days prior to the date shown in the calendar.

The Scholarship Workshop LLC and Marianne Ragins have no control over the quality, safety or legality of the scholarships or awards shown nor the ability of the scholarship and award sponsors/providers to provide scholarships or awards. *The Scholarship Monthly Planner* may contain inaccuracies or typographical errors. The Scholarship Workshop LLC nor Marianne Ragins make no representations concerning the accuracy, reliability, completeness, or timeliness of any information included in *The Scholarship Monthly Planner*. The use of *The Scholarship Monthly Planner* is at your own risk. Changes are periodically made to *The Scholarship Monthly Planner* and may be made at any time.

THE SCHOLARSHIP WORKSHOP LLC DOES NOT WARRANT THAT ANY INFORMATION IN *THE SCHOLARSHIP MONTHLY PLANNER* WILL BE ERROR-FREE. THE CONTENT PROVIDED IN THE SCHOLARSHIP MONTHLY PLANNER IS PROVIDED ON AN "AS IS" BASIS WITHOUT ANY WARRANTIES OF ANY KIND. THE SCHOLARSHIP WORKSHOP LLC AND MARIANNE RAGINS, TO THE FULLEST EXTENT PERMITTED BY LAW, DISCLAIMS ALL WARRANTIES, WHETHER EXPRESS OR IMPLIED, INCLUDING THE WARRANTY OF MERCHANTABILITY, FITNESS FOR PARTICULAR PURPOSE AND NON-INFRINGEMENT. THE SCHOLARSHIP WORKSHOP LLC AND MARIANNE RAGINS MAKE NO WARRANTIES ABOUT THE ACCURACY, RELIABILITY, COMPLETENESS, OR TIMELINESS OF THE MATERIAL, REFERENCES, TEXT, GRAPHICS, AND WEBSITES.

www.ingramcontent.com/pod-product-compliance
Lightning Source LLC
Chambersburg PA
CBHW080429030426
42335CB00020B/2659